To: ______________________________

The Lord your God will be with you wherever you go.
Joshua 1:9

From: ___________________________

A Companion Journal for God Is Closer Than You Think
Copyright © 2005 by John Ortberg
ISBN 0-310-81059-0

At Inspirio, we love to hear from you—your stories, your feedback, and your product ideas. Please send your comments to us by way of email at icares@zondervan.com.

Requests for information should be addressed to:
Inspirio, the gift group of Zondervan
Grand Rapids, Michigan 49530
http://www.inspiriogifts.com

Project Manager: Tom Dean
Design Manager: Val Buick
Designer: Kris Perpich

Printed in the United States of America
05 06 07/DCI/5 4 3 2 1

A COMPANION JOURNAL FOR

GOD IS CLOSER THAN YOU THINK

Chapter 1

God's Great Desire

For over the margins of life comes a whisper, a faint call, a premonition of richer living....

Thomas Kelly

Call upon me in the day of trouble; I will deliver you and you shall glorify me. Ps 50:15

God's Great Desire

In Michelangelo's brilliant painting of God and Adam on the ceiling of the Sistine Chapel, the figure of God is extended toward the man with great vigor. His hand comes within a hair's breath of the hand of the man. God is as close as he can be. But having come that close, he allows just a little space, so that Adam can choose. For nearly half a millennium this picture has spoken of God's great desire to be with the human beings he has made in his own image.

The "Everywhereness" of God

God is closer than we think. He is never farther than a prayer away. All it takes is the barest effort, the lift of a finger. Every moment—this moment right now, as you read these words—is the "one timeless moment" of divine endowment, of life with God.

What small effort can you make today to reach out to God?

Foundational Truth: God is always present and active in my life, whether or not I see him.

God's Great Desire

"This is my Father's world," an old song says. "He shines in all that's fair.... In the rustling grass I can hear him pass, he speaks to me everywhere." The Scriptures are full of what might be called the everywhereness of God's speaking.

The heavens declare the
glory of God;
the skies proclaim
the work of his
hands.
Day after day they pour
forth speech;
night after night
they display
knowledge.

Psalm 19:1–2

God's Great Desire

The story of the Bible demonstrates the desire of God to be with people. One day I was sitting on a plane next to a businessman. The screen saver on his computer was the picture of a towheaded little boy. The man was rushing through the skies, taking a chariot through the clouds, implacably determined to be at home with his child. He didn't simply want to love his son from a distance. He wanted to *be with him.*

How would your relationship with God change if you spent more time being with him than loving him from afar?

Foundational Truth: Coming to recognize and experience God's presence is *learned* behavior; I can cultivate it.

The Primary Promise: I Will Be with You

The central promise in the Bible is not "I will forgive you." It is not even the promise of life after death. The most frequent promise in the Bible is "I will be with you." Before Adam and Eve ever sinned or needed forgiveness, they were promised God's presence. He would walk with them in the cool of the day. The promise came to Enoch, who "walked with God." It was made to Noah, to Abraham and Sarah, to Jacob and Joseph and Moses and David and Amos and Mary and Paul and too many others to list.

Foundational Truth: My task is to meet God in this moment.

God gave Israel the tabernacle and the ark of the covenant, and manna and the temple, and a pillar of cloud and another one of fire, like so many Post-It notes saying, "Don't forget. I am with you." When God himself came to earth, his redemptive name was Immanuel—God with us. When Jesus left, his promise was, "I am with you always, even to the end of the age."

How could you better embrace and remember God's promise to be with you?

Foundational Truth: I am always tempted to live "outside" this moment. When I do that, I lose my sense of God's presence.

"I Can Feel Him Walking Around ..."

An ancient sage named Theophan the Recluse, said, "Find a place in your heart and speak there with the Lord. It is the Lord's reception room." Some people seem to find this room easily. Friends of ours have a daughter who said when she was five years old, "I know Jesus lives in my heart, because when I put my hand on it I can feel him walking around in there."

God's Great Desire

Some people seem to be as aware of God as they are of gravity. Telling them how to look for God would be like telling a fish how to look for water. But I am Adam. My life hinges on the presence of God, for courage and guidance and hope all reside with him. But I am aware of the gap—even if it is only a hairbreadth. And in the midst of all my weakness and occasional spiritual indifference, I long for the touch that will close the gap.

How would you define the gap between you and God?

Foundational Truth: Sometimes God seems far away for reasons I do not understand. Those moments, too, are opportunities to learn.

God with Jacob

Each moment that we live outside the awareness of God's presence is a kind of sleepwalking, which is why Paul wrote, "Wake up, O sleeper, rise from the dead, and Christ will shine on you."

How can you recognize when you are spiritually sleepwalking during the day? What can you do at such times to awaken yourself?

Foundational Truth: Whenever I fail at recognizing and experiencing God's presence, I can always start again right away.

Jacob's most striking phrase is, "and I was not aware of it." Somehow he was looking in the wrong direction. Apparently it is possible for God to be present without the person recognizing that he is there. God could be closer than you think.

What normally alerts you to the presence of God? How can you train yourself to look for him when you are not aware he is near?

Foundational Truth: No one knows the full extent to which a human being can experience God's presence.

God Waving Hello

God is crying out all around us. He is present in the breathless silence of the snow-smothered mountains; he is dancing with the sunlight that shatters on the ocean's waves; he is hiding in the decaying moss and lichen and crumbling shale in the old forgotten places in the world. No jagged mountain throws its sharp weight against the sky that is not a testament to his goodness. The entire sum of Creation, each private and individual act of nature, is God waving hello.

Mallory Ortberg

God's Great Desire

Two early followers of Jesus were walking on the road to Emmaus after the crucifixion. They were joined by a third man. It was Jesus, walking and talking with them—but they didn't know it was him. What if when you are on the road to Emmaus—maybe the road on which you commute to work or school or home—Jesus is walking beside you?

How would you feel if you could see Jesus walking beside you everywhere you went? How would you act?

Foundational Truth: My desire for God ebbs and flows, but his desire for me is constant.

How Close Has God Come?

There is no event so commonplace but that God is not present within it, always hidden, always leaving you room to recognize him or not ... because in the last analysis all moments are key moments, and life itself is grace.

Frederick Buechner

How does God reach out to you in life's ordinary moments? How can you reach out to him?

Foundational Truth: Every thought carries a "spiritual charge" that moves me a little closer to or a little farther from God.

Scripture teaches that God really is present right here, right now. Michelangelo's picture really does express spiritual reality. The Spirit of God is available to you and me: flowing all the time, welling up within us, quenching our unsatisfied desires, overflowing to refresh those around us. He is at work all the time, in every place.

Because God is always present, always working, how can you be always in touch with him, always available to be used by him?

God with the Kitchen Guy

One day Brother Lawrence was looking at a tree, and the same truth struck him that struck the psalmist so long ago: the secret of a tree's life is that it remains rooted in something deeper than itself. He decided to make his life an experiment in what he called a "habitual, silent, secret conversation of the soul with God." Although he remained obscure throughout his life, people around him experienced rivers of living water in his life that drew them closer to God.

Foundational Truth: Every aspect of my life—work, relationships, hobbies, errands—is of immense and genuine interest to God.

Now It's Our Turn

Spiritual growth, in a sense, is simply increasing our capacity to experience the presence of God. Brother Lawrence wrote, "The most holy and necessary practice in our spiritual life is the presence of God. That means finding constant pleasure in His divine company, speaking humbly and lovingly with him in all seasons, at every moment, without limiting the conversation in any way."

What limits your conversation with God? How can you help the communication flow more freely?

Foundational Truth: My path to experiencing God's presence will not look exactly like anyone else's.

God's Great Desire

No one has ever lived with a sense of the presence of God as Jesus did. The river of life flowed through him stronger than it had ever flowed through anyone before him. And when he died, the veil to the Holy of Holies—the veil that symbolized separation between God and human beings—was torn in two. In Jesus, God touched Adam.

Foundational Truth: I can experience God's presence without straining and trying too hard.

Chapter 2

Where's Waldo?

We may ignore, but we cannot evade, the presence of God. The world is crowded with him. He walks everywhere incognito. And the incognito is not always easy to penetrate. The real labor is to remember to attend.

Armand Nicholi

Where's Waldo?

On Michelangelo's ceiling, all Adam has to do is lift a finger and he can touch the hand of God. God is that close. Yet it's not that simple—not for me, anyway. Sometimes I wish God would show himself more plainly. He is, after all, invisible, inaudible, and untouchable. Sometimes I lift a finger; sometimes I really do try, but not much seems to happen.

Foundational Truth: God is always present and active in my life, whether or not I see him.

Where's Waldo?

"Sometimes He Hides Himself"

More than 40 million "Where's Waldo" books have been sold in twenty-eight countries. This guy Waldo is supposed to be on every page. The author assures us that it is so. But he is often hidden to the untrained eye. You have to be willing to look for him. When you find him, there is a sense of joy and accomplishment. In fact, developing the capacity to track him down is part of the point of the book. The difficulty of the task is what increases the power of discernment.

How can the anticipation of joy help you overcome the difficulty of discerning God's presence?

Foundational Truth: Coming to recognize and experience God's presence is learned behavior; I can cultivate it.

Where's Waldo?

Let every day, every moment, of your life be another page. God is there—on every one of them—but the ease with which he may be found varies from one page to the next. Brother Lawrence wrote, "God has various ways of drawing us to him, but sometimes he hides himself."

How do you react when God seems to be hiding from you? Does your reaction draw you closer to him or push you farther away?

Foundational Truth:
My task is to meet God in *this* moment.

Where's Waldo?

Rainbow Days

On rainbow days God's presence is hard to miss. Your life is filled with too much goodness and meaning for you to believe it is simply by chance. You find yourself wanting to pray, believing that God hears, open to receiving and acting on his response. God seems to speak personally to you through Scripture. People who are wise learn to treasure rainbow days as gifts. They store them up to remember on days when God seems more elusive.

How can you treasure rainbow days more? How can you better recall them on rainy days?

Where's Waldo?

Waldo is generally easiest to find on the earliest pages. The farther you get into the book, the harder he is to locate. Something like this often goes on in spiritual life. St. John of the Cross wrote that often when someone first becomes a Christian, God fills them with a desire to seek him: They want to read Scripture, they are eager to pray, they are filled with a desire to serve. After a while, this initial eagerness wears off. God takes away the props so that we can begin to grow true devotion that is strong enough to carry on even when unaided by emotions.

Foundational Truth: I am always tempted to live "outside" this moment. When I do that, I lose my sense of God's presence.

Where's Waldo?

Ordinary Days

During some eras of spiritual life we fall into a kind of maintenance mode. Life becomes routine. At this time there is not a major crisis, no obvious problems, but no major gains either. We may feel as if we're in a spiritual rut. We do not experience being in the flow with God. Waldo is still present on these pages of our lives. We can find him, if we remember to look. But we're apt not to notice him. Our attention is elsewhere.

How can you remember to seek God when your spiritual life seems ordinary and other things appear more exciting?

> **Foundational Truth:** Sometimes God seems far away for reasons I do not understand. Those moments, too, are opportunities to learn.

Spiritual Habituation

When a new object or stimulus is introduced to our environment, we are intensely aware of it, but the awareness fades over time. For example, at first we feel a new watch on our wrist constantly, but after a while we don't even notice it's there. Psychologists refer to this phenomenon as "habituation." One of the greatest challenges in life is fighting what might be called spiritual habituation. We have a kind of spiritual attention deficit disorder that God must break through.

Foundational Truth: Whenever I fail to recognize and experience God's presence, I can always start again right away.

Where's Waldo?

Whether we are aware of it or not, at every moment of our existence we are encountering God, Father, Son, and Holy Spirit, who is trying to catch our attention, trying to draw us into a reciprocal conscious relationship.

William Barry

Can you identify the things in your life that are drawing your focus away from God?

Foundational Truth: No one knows the full extent to which a human being can experience God's presence.

Where's Waldo?

Reviewing the Dailies

It's very helpful to take a few moments to walk through yesterday in your mind with God and ask where he was present and at work in each scene. As I review what happened when I greeted my family, ate breakfast, and went through meetings at work, I realize God was talking to me through the words of another person or the lines of a book or the therapy of laughter. The more often I review, the better I get at recognizing him in "real time."

Foundational Truth: My desire for God ebbs and flows, but his desire for me is constant.

Where's Waldo?

Spiritual Hiding

Sometimes we don't have much of a sense for God's presence in our lives, but there's really no mystery to it. The truth is, our desire for God can be pretty selective. Sometimes we don't want God to be around. Anytime we choose to do wrong or to not do right, we choose hiddenness. It may be that out of all the prayers that are ever spoken, the most common one—the quietest one, the one that we least acknowledge—is simply this: Don't look at me, God.

What can you do to remind yourself, when you are tempted, that choosing sin will force you to hide from God?

Where's Waldo?

The Law of the Oatmeal Brush

As long as I tried to maintain the lie, a strange dynamic was at work in my spirit. I had to muster up enough anger and hurt and pride to justify my deceit. I had to cut myself off from humility and truth. I had to pray, *Don't look at me, God.* But when I confessed the truth, I could quit hiding. I could see Waldo on the page again. *The Law of the Oatmeal Brush is that every choice to sin—no matter how small—diminishes my capacity to experience God.*

Foundational Truth: Every thought carries a "spiritual charge" that moves me a little closer to or a little farther from God.

Where's Waldo?

When God Seems AWOL

Sometimes I cannot find Waldo, no matter how hard I try. Sometimes it seems that God cannot be found even though we really want to find him. I have had times when I tried to pray—really tried—and my prayers seemed to bounce off the ceiling. I think of days when I have carried a ball of anxiety in my belly, asking God to send peace, yet the pain remained.

To what passages of Scripture do you turn when God seems distant? What else helps you?

The Good of Not Knowing

Imagine for a moment two football teams walking onto the field, knowing ahead of time what the final score of the game is going to be. It would be hard to get much adrenaline going. Uncertainty is essential to the game. Welcome to the human race. It is somehow essential to human life as God has ordained it that we can know the final score of yesterday, but not to-morrow.

Foundational Truth: Every aspect of my life—work, relationships, hobbies, errands—is of immense and genuine interest to God.

God Where You Least Expect Him

You have to trust the Author. You have to believe that God has a good reason for keeping his presence subtle. It allows creatures as small and frail as human beings the capacity for choice that we would never have in the obvious presence of infinite power. God wants to be known, but not in a way that overwhelms us, that takes away the possibility of love freely chosen.

What about your experience with God in the past gives you confidence to trust him today?

Foundational Truth: My path to experiencing God's presence will not look quite like anyone else's.

Where's Waldo?

The image of God that Michelangelo created became famous. It speaks something of the kind of majesty and dignity and strength we associate with the God of the universe. But when God did come down to be with us—Immanuel—he did not look like that. It's as if he put on Waldo's goofy-looking glasses and a striped shirt. He looked ordinary.

Foundational Truth: I can experience God's presence without straining and trying too hard.

Chapter 3 Life with God

Life with God

Who [in the Bible] besides Jesus really knew which end was up? Nobody.... Jesus realized there is no separation from God.

J.D. Salinger

A Spiritual D.T.R.

A "Define the Relationship" conversation is a call for relational clarity. In Jesus' day, being in relationship with him inevitably involved having a spiritual D.T.R. Jesus gently but relentlessly asked people to make a decision about their relationship with him, giving this invitation: Follow me. Come be with me, and learn from me how to be like me. Jesus himself called this decision choosing "the one thing needful."

How would you define your relationship with Jesus?

Foundational Truth: God is always present and active in my life, whether or not I see him.

Life with God

It's Not about Personality Types

The story about Martha and Mary is often misunderstood to be about two different personality types. People often wrongly assume it teaches that God's presence requires us to stop doing things. But Jesus has a lot to say about doing. The last thing he told his closest friends was to go throughout the world, devoting themselves to making disciples and teaching them to do everything he commanded. That turned out to be a lot of work. And it would be precisely in that doing, Jesus promised, that "I will be with you always."

In what ways are you like Mary? In what ways are you like Martha? How does your unique personality help and hinder your relationship with Jesus?

Life with God

To a mother with young children, words like stillness and solitude seem foreign. But is it God's plan that a busy mother should experience his presence less than a hermit in a cave? One of the great barriers to practicing God's presence is the belief that our temperament or the demands and activity of daily life inevitably interfere with our living in the presence of Jesus.

Foundational Truth: Coming to recognize and experience God's presence is learned behavior; I can cultivate it.

Life with God

"Sitting at the Lord's Feet"

Mary "sat at the Lord's feet." This is not just a description of her location in the room. It is an assertion that Mary has made the fundamental decision of her life. To "sit at someone's feet" was a technical expression in ancient times to indicate the relationship between a disciple and a rabbi. To make someone your rabbi was to make a choice to be with him. A disciple was someone who had chosen to "be with" his rabbi and learn everything he could from him.

Are you a true disciple of Jesus? What evidence do you see in your life that shows you are committed to being with him as much as possible?

Life with God

"The Dust of Your Rabbi"

Disciples never wanted to let their rabbi out of their sight. Every activity was an opportunity to learn from the rabbi how to be like the rabbi. I can be "sitting at Jesus' feet" when I'm kneeling in prayer or negotiating a contract or fixing my kids lunch or watching a movie. All it requires is asking him to be my teacher and companion in this moment.

Into which daily activities are you willing to invite Jesus? Which do you feel you can handle on your own?

Foundational Truth: My task is to meet God in this moment.

Life with God

First-century Jews had a blessing that beautifully expresses the commitment of a disciple to stay in the presence of the one he followed: "May you always be covered by the dust of your rabbi." What if you were to wake up each morning and begin with this prayer: *Today I would like to be covered in the dust of my rabbi?* Jesus has made God's presence available to anyone who wants it. Male or female, young or old, hermit or homemaker, peasant or king.

Foundational Truth: I am always tempted to live "outside" this moment. When I do that, I lose my sense of God's presence.

The Fundamental Obstacle

Luke alerts us to the great obstacle that keeps us from being with Jesus when he says that Martha was "distracted" by all the preparations. She wasn't too "busy." She wasn't "overcommitted." His word is distracted—a word sometimes used as meaning to be physically pulled or dragged away from something. The implication is that Martha had wanted to be with Jesus; that was her initial intent. But she allowed herself to be prevented from doing that by the pressure of providing hospitality.

What distracts you the most from being with Jesus?

Foundational Truth: Sometimes God seems far away for reasons I do not understand. Those moments, too, are opportunities to learn.

Life with God

"One Thing Is Needed"

Sometimes "sitting at Jesus' feet" means we must stop doing what we have been doing and start doing something else. Maybe we have been driving ourselves to the point of exhaustion, and sitting at Jesus' feet means we have to trust him enough to get some sleep. Maybe we have been watching television while our spouse washes the dishes, and at that moment the dust of the rabbi is all in the kitchen. However, as a general rule we don't need to switch activities in order to be with Jesus. All we need to do is invite him into whatever we are doing at the moment.

What do you need to stop doing so you can sit at Jesus' feet?

Life with God

What keeps someone from Jesus' presence is not just busyness—having a lot of things to do. It's distraction. Martha wasn't doing bad things. She wasn't breaking the Ten Commandments or gossiping about her neighbors or spending hours watching the a shopping channel on TV and ordering stuff with somebody else's credit card. Martha wasn't sinning. She simply wasn't being with Jesus.

Foundational Truth: Whenever I fail at recognizing and experiencing God's presence, I can always start again right away.

"Distracted, Worried, Upset"

Martha experiences the great obstacle that keeps many of us today from being covered with the dust of the rabbi. Martha is distracted from noticing and basking in Jesus' presence, and therefore she becomes worried and upset by many things. Not defiant. Not hate-filled. Not rebellious. Just distracted, worried, upset. Same house, different rooms.

What is your spiritual state of mind most of the time? How does this reflect whether you are distracted or enjoying Jesus' presence?

Foundational Truth: No one knows the full extent to which a human being can experience God's presence.

Life with God

Jesus says, "Mary has chosen what is better." He is saying in effect, "The truth is, Martha, the real banquet going on here is the one I want to serve to you. Mary has chosen the best dish of all."

When you consider the choices you have made in life, both the big ones and the little ones, do you think you have chosen what is better? In what ways could poor choices in small matters be affecting your spiritual life?

Foundational Truth: My desire for God ebbs and flows, but his desire for me is constant.

The Art of Letting Go

Sometimes in our Martha moments, we live under the illusion that worry enhances our ability to control the world. We worry as if we're in control of something that's actually completely out of our hands. When I bowl, certain things are up to me. But once the ball is headed down the alley, I've done all I can do. The secret for more joy-filled bowling is, When you let it go—let it go.

In what areas of your life do you need to let go? When you're tempted to worry again, how will you remind yourself that God's now in control?

To let go is not the same thing as simply resigning oneself to whatever circumstances come along. "Sitting at Jesus' feet" does not mean passivity. Jesus desires that we be active, choosing, risking, stretching, and doing. But we must also recognize that he is present here and now, and we don't have to pretend we control the universe.

Foundational Truth: Every thought carries a "spiritual charge" that moves me a little closer to or a little farther from God.

The great danger of worry is that it keeps me upset in the kitchen instead of sitting at the feet of the One who loves me. If I find I've been worrying, I don't beat myself up or say, "I'll try harder to not worry." The single most powerful step I can take to combat worry is to seek to be covered with the dust of my rabbi. Worry is a reminder to have another D.T.R., a kind of prickly invitation to sit at Jesus' feet.

What other negative emotions can remind you to have a spiritual D.T.R. with Jesus?

Foundational Truth: Every aspect of my life—work, relationships, hobbies, errands—is of immense and genuine interest to God.

Growing No Faster "Than Grace Allows"

Part of life we may spend, as Mary did, in the living room during times of quiet and peace. But much of life will be spent "in the kitchen with Martha"—in our place of work. Jesus will come into the kitchen—if we ask him. Brother Lawrence spent most of his adult life in the kitchen. He called himself "the lord of all pots and pans" because he never went any higher on the organizational chart than cook and bottle-washer. But he learned how to make his tasks an exercise in sitting at Jesus' feet because he chose the one thing needful.

Foundational Truth: My path to experiencing God's presence will not look quite like anyone else's.

Life with God

If you find yourself slow in making progress, take heart. Brother Lawrence writes that for ten years, "I was worried that my walk with the Lord wasn't good enough." He finally reached a point where he stopped expecting to grow any faster, and he was at last able to begin to live in grace from one moment to the next. He counseled others to be similarly patient, to not desire to "go faster than grace allows."

What can you do to develop patience in your spiritual journey?

Foundational Truth: I can experience God's presence without straining and trying too hard.

Chapter 4 The Greatest Moment of Your Life

To see a world in a grain
of sand
And a heaven in a wild
flower,
Hold infinity in the
palm of your
hand
And eternity in an hour.
William Blake

The Greatest Moment of Your Life

The greatest moment of your life is this moment right now. This tick of the clock. This beat of your heart. Not because it's pleasant or happy or easy, but because this moment is the only moment you've got. This moment is God's irreplaceable gift to you. Most of all, this is the moment that matters, because this moment is where God is. If you are going to be with God at all, you must be with him *now.*

How comfortable are you with meeting with God anytime, coming to him just as you are? How could you learn to better receive his grace?

> This is the day the Lord
> has made;
> let us rejoice and be
> glad in it.
> **Psalm 118:24**

The Sacrament of the Present Moment

A sacrament, according to church tradition, is a "means of grace." It is an ordinary object—the water used in baptism, the cup of communion—that somehow becomes a vessel of the extraordinary, of the divine. Jean Pierre de Caussade, author of *The Sacrament of the Present Moment*, says that each moment of our lives can be a sacrament, a vehicle for God's love and power. In the same way that every lungful of air gives life to our bodies, every moment in time can—if we learn to let it—give life to our souls.

Foundational Truth: God is *always* present and active in my life, whether or not I see him.

Morning, afternoon, evening—the hours of the day, of any day, of your day and my day. The alphabet of grace. If there is a God who speaks anywhere, surely he speaks here: through waking up and working, through going away and coming back again, through people you read and books you meet, through falling asleep in the dark.

Frederick Buechner

At what time of day, or during which of your daily activities, do you most sense God's presence?

Foundational Truth: Coming to recognize and experience God's presence is learned behavior; I can cultivate it.

The Greatest Danger

If this is the greatest moment of life, I want to suggest what might be the single most dangerous word in the English language. It is found in a story out of the book of Exodus. When Pharaoh asks Moses to pray to remove the plague of frogs, Moses tells him to set the time. And Pharaoh answers in a single word: "Tomorrow." There's the dangerous word: *tomorrow. Let's wait until tomorrow*.

Foundational Truth: My task is to meet God in *this* moment.

Motivated Irrationality

People persistently tolerate and maintain behavioral patterns that will destroy their lives. This has puzzled the human race a long time. The Greeks were big into reason, and they couldn't figure out why human beings choose to repeatedly engage in such irrational acts. The Greeks called this akrasia, believing that the gods clouded human thinking and led humans to do crazy things.

What irrational things do you do, and why do you think you do them?

Foundational Truth: I am always tempted to live "outside" this moment. When I do that, I lose my sense of God's presence.

Eternity in Disguise

Tomorrow may cause us to mismanage finances; it may mean problems at work; it can damage relationships; it can eat up our self-esteem and erode our joy. But none of these scenarios gets to the root of the problem. What matters most is this: God is present in this instant, offering to partner with us in whatever we face. The failure to embrace "the sacrament of the present moment" will keep us from being fully present to God right here, right now. Not because we consciously say no to God. We just say, "Tomorrow." Spiritual *akrasia*. Another night with the frogs.

Foundational Truth: Sometimes God seems far away for reasons I do not understand. Those moments, too, are opportunities to learn.

The Greatest Moment of Your Life

We think the great adventure of partnership with God lies somewhere in the future. We tell ourselves that we will grow closer to God someday when our kids are no longer small and demanding, or when the pressures of work lighten up, or when we become more disciplined, or when our motivation level is higher, or when we just magically grow into spiritual maturity. "God is closer than you think" means he is available in *this moment, right now.* Always now. Only now.

What practical things can you do to remind yourself that the time to experience God is always now?

Foundational Truth: Whenever I fail at recognizing and experiencing God's presence, I can always start again right away.

The Day Starts at Night

In Western culture we think of a day beginning when the sun comes up. But the ancient rhythm of days is different. In the creation account, each day begins with evening. In Jewish life, the Sabbath begins not at sunup but at sundown. Eugene Peterson notes that in this way the biblical writers help us to remember: Everything doesn't depend on me. I go to sleep, God goes to work. It's his day. The world keeps spinning, tides ebb and flow, lives begin and end—even though I am not there to superintend any of it. God is present when I sleep.

Those who have the wind of the Holy Spirit in the sails glide ahead even while asleep.

Brother Lawrence

Remember what happened to the disciples in the garden of Gethsemane when Jesus wanted them to pray? They slept. But another time, when they were on the boat in a storm and Jesus was sleeping, they were wide awake with worry and fear. Their problem was that they slept when they should have been awake, stayed awake when they should have slept. They had a sleep disorder.

Do you have a spiritual sleep disorder? How can you become a better disciple of Jesus by learning to sleep when you should sleep, and stay awake when you should stay awake?

Foundational Truth: No one knows the full extent to which a human being can experience God's presence.

Waking

Sometimes people who are not "morning people" put pressure on themselves to have extended times reading Scripture or praying first thing in the morning. If this is effective for you, great. If not, try to arrange—as early as you can after you wake up—to have just a few minutes alone with God. Do three things: Acknowledge your dependence on God. Tell him about your concerns for the day, asking him to identify and remove any fear in you. And renew your invitation for God to spend the day with you.

> In the morning I lay my requests before you and wait in expectation.
> **Psalm 5:3**

Getting Ready

In ancient times, cleansing and purification were a very important and highly symbolic part of life. Priests had to go through a very elaborate process of cleansing before entering the temple. This served as a reminder of the need for our souls to be cleansed. Tomorrow morning, when you are washing your face or taking a shower, make it a moment of prayer: *God, just as this soap and water are cleaning my body, may your Word and your Spirit cleanse my mind and heart.*

How would you rewrite this cleansing prayer in your own words to make it more real and meaningful to you?

Foundational Truth: My desire for God ebbs and flows, but his desire for me is constant.

Eating

Food is a gift from God. To the writers of Scripture, food is concrete evidence that God is present and providing. Make mealtimes an exercise in gratitude. Stop and notice your food. Remember God's goodness to you, and thank him. Jesus said that we do "not live on bread alone, but on every word that comes from the mouth of God." As our bodies are fed by food, so our spirits are fed by words with ideas and images. We are flooded by words that can mislead us, so we need to feed our minds each day with the Word of God.

Foundational Truth: Every thought carries a "spiritual charge" that moves me a little closer to or a little farther from God.

Working

Work is perhaps the single most important activity to learn to do together with Jesus. I generally start work by reviewing my meetings and tasks for the day, and—instead of worrying about them—asking God if we can partner together in them. Every few hours I try to remember to take a break. That may be something as simple as sitting up straight and taking a few deep breaths; as I breathe, I remember that I am being filled with God's Spirit. I may look out the window at something growing outside, or listen to music that speaks to my soul.

Practically and realistically, what things could you regularly do during your workday to allow God's Spirit to refresh you?

Interruptions

It is possible that when the phone rings or there's a knock on the door or somebody wants a favor or I see a person with a flat tire on the side of the road, it is a divine appointment. God has come close. What would Jesus' ministry have looked like if he had never allowed himself to be interrupted? Many of his greatest miracles and most unforgettable encounters were the result of Spirit-prompted interruptions. Even the cross—which looked like the ultimate interruption of his ministry—was in fact the greatest work his Father had for him to do.

Foundational Truth: Every aspect of my life—work, relationships, hobbies, errands—is of immense and genuine interest to God.

Odds and Ends

Then there are all the moments that don't fit into any particular category: paying bills and running errands and greeting those you live with when you come home from work. All these can become moments of companionship. Pick an ordinary day when you will actually try this "with-God" experiment. Don't attempt to do a lot of new heroic things. Do the things you normally do—only do them with God. Because if you can spend one ordinary day with Jesus, you can spend every day with him. One day at a time.

Which everyday activities will you turn into "with-God" events, and how?

Foundational Truth: My path to experiencing God's presence will not look quite like anyone else's.

The Greatest Moment of Your Life

In our culture we often talk about "embracing the moment" and "seizing the day." Although these ideas express a deep longing in our hearts, they are not powerful enough to transform us. We were not meant to embrace moments, because moments and days, like the pages of a newspaper, can be filled with bad news as well as good. Rather, we are meant to embrace God. Moments are not always good; God is nothing but good. Moments are simply the place where we meet him.

Foundational Truth: I can experience God's presence without straining and trying too hard.

Chapter 5

A Beautiful Mind

A mystic is anyone who believes that, when you talk to God, God talks back.

Frank Laubach

A Beautiful Mind

In the movie *A Beautiful Mind*, we see the characters and hear the voices that exist only in John Nash's head, unconnected to reality. What makes his story so remarkable is that he was actually able to learn, over time, the art of discernment. He learned to test the voices, to find out which ones were false and which ones were true. Nash speaks at one point in the film about how in a way his battle is the battle of all of us. "I'm not so different from you," he says to his friend. "We all hear voices. We just have to decide which ones we are going to listen to."

What voices do you hear? How do you determine to which you should listen?

A Beautiful Mind

"We All Hear Voices"

Two people live in a universe where God is always present. One of them decides that "in all my thoughts there is no room for God." The other says, "Always before me I set you, O Lord." God's offer of availability is the same. The difference is in their minds. The mind is an instrument of staggering potential. But its potential is not measured by IQ or academic degrees. It is in our minds that we live in conscious awareness of and interaction with God.

Foundational Truth: God is always present and active in my life, whether or not I see him.

A Beautiful Mind

"We all hear voices...." At least I do. Some of them are distorted and destructive, speaking envy and resentment and fear. Some of them are healthy and strong, speaking words of love and truth. The ones I listen to shape my life. But there's one Voice above all to which we're called to listen. Jesus said that he is the Good Shepherd and that "his sheep follow him because they know his voice." Throughout history, those who have practiced God's presence most have insisted that they hear his voice. They have learned, so to speak, to program their minds to be constantly receiving the divine channel.

What practical steps can you take to better recognize Jesus' voice?

I Must Believe That God Really Will Speak to Me

God can speak to us through Scripture, of course, or through the words of another person. But he also has "direct access;" he can plant a thought directly in our minds. Anytime. Anywhere. It is possible that any given thought that runs through our minds might have been placed there by God—and we may not even know it. This means that if we are to meet God at all, the place where we dwell with him will be in our minds. Thoughts happen. And some of those thoughts come from God.

Foundational Truth: Coming to recognize and experience God's presence is learned behavior; I can cultivate it.

I Recognize That I Cannot Control His Speaking

There is much about God's speaking that is a mystery to me. But one thing is certain: There are no formulas. I cannot control God's communicating with me. I cannot force him to speak through my piety, sincerity, or hard work. I cannot force God to give me the guidance or help I think I need. There may be a good reason for his remaining silent sometimes. At the human level, wise parents and good friends often recognize the need for silence, so surely at the divine level, God does as well.

How can you stop trying to compel God to speak to you, and instead begin inviting him to speak?

A Beautiful Mind

God knows me well enough to know that if I have to grapple with decisions—to think and struggle and examine my motives and assess the future and have conversations with wise friends and take responsibility for choices—I will grow in ways that would never be possible if I simply received a postcard with directions from him in the mail. And God's primary concern for me is not my external situation—it's the kind of person I'm becoming.

Foundational Truth: My task is to meet God in *this* moment.

A Beautiful Mind

Every Thought Holds the Promise of Carrying Me into God's Presence

All our thoughts carry with them a kind of spiritual charge. When the Holy Spirit is present and at work in a human mind, he always moves it in the direction of life. On the other hand, the mind that shuts itself off to the presence of God tends toward destructiveness. Each thought we have carries with it a little spiritual power, a tug toward or away from God.

Do your thoughts generally take you closer to God or farther from him? How can you take better control of your thought life?

Foundational Truth: I am always tempted to live "outside" this moment. When I do that, I lose my sense of God's presence.

A Beautiful Mind

Every thought is either enabling and strengthening you to live a kingdom kind of life, or robbing you of that life. Every thought is—at least to a small extent—God-breathed or God-avoidant; leading to death or leading toward life. In time, if we listen carefully, we can learn to recognize his voice. Not infallibly, of course. But the kind of thoughts that come from God are those in line with the fruit of the Spirit; they move us toward love and joy and peace and patience.

Foundational Truth: Sometimes God seems far away for reasons I do not understand. Those moments, too, are opportunities to learn.

Saying "Yes" When He Speaks

For who is so devoid of intellect as not to understand that God, in so speaking, lisps with us as nurses are wont to do with little children?... In doing so, he must, of course, stoop far below his proper height.

John Calvin

God is gracious to communicate to us even at the point of our immaturity in a way that we can understand. God stoops. God lisps. Our job is to be ruthless about saying yes when we believe God is speaking to us. Every time we do, we will become more sensitive to hearing him the next time. Our mind becomes a little more receptive, a little more tuned in to God's channel.

A Beautiful Mind

The "Without-God" Mind

When people are alone, undistracted by noise or activity, their minds naturally drift toward an awareness of discontentment, a sense of inadequacy, anxiety about the future, or a chronic sense of self-preoccupation. This is why people generally flee solitude. But God never desires that our minds be filled with despair or tormented by unsatisfied longings. God's desire is for us to have a mind permeated by life-giving thoughts.

What practical steps can you take, when you are alone, to empty your mind of negative, destructive thoughts and fill it with healthy, positive ones?

Foundational Truth: Whenever I fail at recognizing and experiencing God's presence, I can always start again right away.

Only God Can Change a Mind

Paul wrote to the church at Rome to "be transformed by the renewing of your minds." He didn't say "transform yourselves by renewing your minds." Only God can change a mind. When God is present in a mind, it begins to flow with a new kind of thought. But there is a role for us to play. We can, by choice and by our actions, invite God to be present in our minds. Or we can close the door to him. It all depends on what kind of minds we want to cultivate.

Foundational Truth: No one knows the full extent to which a human being can experience God's presence.

A Beautiful Mind

Make your mind the dwelling place of God. The goal is to have a mind in which the glorious Father of Jesus is always present and gradually crowds out every distorted belief, every destructive feeling, every misguided intent. You will know your mind is increasingly "set on God" when the moods that dominate your inner life are love, joy, and peace—the three primary components of the fruit of the Spirit.

How can you use the armor of God (Ephesians 6) to help you win the battle in your mind?

Finally, brothers and sisters, whatever is true, whatever is noble, whatever is right, whatever is pure, whatever is lovely, whatever is admirable—if anything is excellent or praiseworthy—think about such things.

Philippians 4:8 TNIV

A Beautiful Mind

Whatever repeatedly enters your mind occupies it, eventually shapes it, and will ultimately express itself in what you do and who you become. The events we attend, the material we read (or don't), the music we listen to, the images we watch, the conversations we hold, the daydreams we entertain—these shape our minds. And ultimately they make our minds deaf or receptive toward the still small voice of God.

Foundational Truth: My desire for God ebbs and flows, but his desire for me is constant.

A Beautiful Mind

Leaning into Community

Often God uses other people to help us discern his voice. There are certain people in your life whose words consistently guide you toward truth and joy and love. Be sure you make time for those people. John Nash learned to lean into community to discern which voices were worth listening to and which were delusional. We can do that as well. *The spirit of Jesus speaks through the community of Jesus.* When you are not sure about a voice, go to some trusted friends and discuss it. Lean into community.

Which people in your life help you hear God? How can you make more time for them?

Foundational Truth: Every aspect of my life—work, relationships, hobbies, errands—is of immense and genuine interest to God.

A Beautiful Mind

Learning to Listen

If we are serious about interactive awareness of God, it means we will have to spend some time listening for him. Listening can involve a variety of practices: reading, solitude and silence, conversations, watching the beauty of a sunset, listening to great music. Perhaps the oldest and most powerful practice is meditation on Scripture. What makes a mind great—what makes a *beautiful mind*—is stored goodness that overflows into a beautiful life.

His delight is in the law
of the Lord,
and on his law he
meditates day and
night.

Psalm 1:2

Foundational Truth: My path to experiencing God's presence will not look quite like anyone else's.

Chapter 6

Waldo Junior

Christ addresses me in the voice of each person I meet.

Esther de Waal

Waldo Junior

Isaiah cried out to God, "Oh, that you would rend the heavens and come down!" And one day God did. How could Isaiah have known—how can any of us know—what "coming down" would cost God? The story of incarnation is the story of love. Many people didn't recognize him as God, of course. They were looking for someone a little flashier. They expected more in the way of special effects, not someone who would take on all our limitations. He came as Waldo.

Do you think you would have recognized Jesus as God if you had been around when he walked the earth? Why or why not?

Foundational Truth: God is *always* present and active in my life, whether or not I see him.

Waldo Junior

Waldo Junior

Initially Jesus was present on earth through the body that was conceived in Mary's womb. But after the ascension he became present on earth through another body—the community of his followers. It's as if there were a second incarnation. The church is, in a sense, Waldo Junior. Of course, it can be even harder to recognize God's presence in the second Waldo than it was in the first one.

Foundational Truth: Coming to recognize and experience God's presence is learned behavior; I can cultivate it.

Waldo Junior

In some way we don't fully understand, God has incarnated himself again. He is present to us through people: a real estate agent, a bank teller, a next-door neighbor, a homeless man. However, most of us don't see. When it comes to people, it is perhaps supremely true that *God is closer than you think*.

Jesus said, "Where two or three are gathered together in my name, there am I in the midst of them."

Matthew 18:20 ASV

In what ways are you prevented from recognizing God's presence in people around you? What can you do about this?

Foundational Truth: My task is to meet God in *this* moment.

Waldo Junior

The Case of Naaman

In Scripture God often mediates his presence and sends his messages through people. One of the classic examples of this involves a man named Naaman, generalissimo of the army of Aram. But he has leprosy, and he's going to die. God doesn't send Naaman a burning bush or a choir of angels. He speaks to him through a slave girl, a prophet's intern, and a lowly servant, telling him, "Go, wash yourself seven times in the Jordan, and you will be cleansed." God sends his message through people.

Foundational Truth: I am always tempted to live "outside" this moment. When I do that, I lose my sense of God's presence.

God says in effect, "Naaman, I'll meet you—if you'll let me. But I will choose the place. What I'm going to ask you to do is not glamorous or impressive. You will have to listen for me in the voice of those you think are less smart and powerful than you. You'll have to meet me at the Jordan." So Naaman goes down to the river. The great general strips off his armor and washes in the Jordan. And there he meets God.

In what ways are you trying too hard to meet God? How can you better trust him to meet you in his ways, even if they seem ordinary to you?

Washing in the Jordan

Let "washing in the Jordan" stand for all our mundane, nonglamorous interactions with people in our lives: going to meetings, reading to a child, listening to a cranky in-law, chatting with a neighbor; doing business with a clerk at a grocery store, gathering with a small group. "Washing in the Jordan" is how we spend most of life. How well do I do looking for God's presence and listening for his messages in the people who were created in his image?

Foundational Truth: I can experience God's presence without straining and trying too hard.

Waldo Junior

Psychologist Henry Cloud was wrestling with depression. He asked God for healing, hoping for something spectacular. Instead, God placed him in a community of people who loved and cared for him. Over time, their support and truthfulness were used for his healing. Henry had thought the "special effects" route was God's Plan A and that people were Plan B. But he realized that with God it is the other way around. People are God's preferred messengers, God's Plan A, because they alone carry his image.

How can you become more open to whatever methods God chooses to answer your prayers?

Foundational Truth: Whenever I fail at recognizing and experiencing God's presence, I can always start again right away.

Waldo Junior

Throughout the Sistine Chapel the faces and bodies of human beings are painted to echo the strength and beauty of God himself. They are "manifestations of human dignity reflecting the divine." Michelangelo himself described human beings as the veils through whom we see God himself.

God, in his grace, shows himself nowhere more
To me, than through some veil, mortal and lovely,
Which I will love for being his mirror.

Michelangelo

Foundational Truth: No one knows the full extent to which a human being can experience God's presence.

God's Preferred Dwelling Place

This doesn't mean, however, that God is particularly present in people whom our society regards as "godlike:" the wealthy and beautiful and strong. On the contrary, as one writer puts it, "Jesus frequently chose the humble, poor, rejected, and despised. They are often the preferred dwelling place of God—in them, we may meet God."

In what ways is it easy for you to believe that Jesus is present, as he said, in the "least of these" (Matthew 25:40)? In what ways is it difficult for you to accept this?

Foundational Truth: My desire for God ebbs and flows, but his desire for me is constant.

Waldo Junior

Mother Teresa once told those working with her to be especially tender when they dealt with the poorest of the poor; when they dealt with the dying and the abandoned on the streets of Calcutta. She told them to treat the poor with the kind of reverence with which a priest handles the elements of the Mass. When you touch them, she said, "there you touch Jesus in his distressing disguise."

Foundational Truth: Every thought carries a "spiritual charge" that moves me a little closer to or a little farther from God.

Waldo Junior

Jesus' parable about the sheep and the goats is at its heart a kind of Waldo parable. The King thanks one group of people and condemns another, based on whether or not they gave him food when he was hungry, something to drink when he was thirsty, clothes when he was ragged, and so on. In both cases the people reply in response, "When did we ever see you in such condition?" The King replies, "Whatever you did for the least of these brothers of mine, you did for me." *God is closer than you think.*

How can you better learn to recognize God's presence in those who are needy?

Waldo Junior

The CIHU Prayer

Frank Laubach wrote of a method of continually experiencing God in interactions with other people through what he called the "CIHU" prayer—standing for "Can I help you?" This one prayer can set a powerful dynamic of God's action in motion.

One speaks to God and man at the same moment asking, "Can I help you get together?" We do not ask, "Do I like you?" or, "Do I need you?" or, "Do I despise you?" but only, "Can I help you?" and, "Can I help you find God?"

Frank Laubach

Foundational Truth: Every aspect of my life—work, relationships, hobbies, errands—is of immense and genuine interest to God.

Waldo Junior

Look and listen for God in each person you see. When you run into a difficult person, hear Jesus saying, “Love your enemies, and pray for those who persecute you.” When you run into a needy person, hear Jesus saying, “Whatever you did for one of the least of these....” When you see someone you love, allow God to love you through them. When someone confronts you, ask God if perhaps he is speaking through them. When you see a stranger, remember the CIHU prayer. When you see a fellow believer, hear Jesus saying, “Where two or three are gathered together in my name, there am I....”

How can you perceive God’s image in every human being? What can you do to see it more clearly?

Waldo Junior

We take long trips to see marvels like the Grand Canyon. Engaged couples plan far ahead so they can honeymoon at Niagara Falls. But if our eyes could see clearly, if our hearts were working right, we would fall to the ground in amazement at the sight of a single human being. They are the miracles. They are the God-carriers. And don't forget to hold your breath in wonder the next time you go into a church. What you gaze on is not just a group of people singing songs or listening to a message. It is God's Body on earth. It's Waldo Junior.

Foundational Truth: My path to experiencing God's presence will not look quite like anyone else's.

Chapter 7

Spiritual Pathways

Why else were individuals created, but that God, loving all infinitely, should love each differently?

C.S. Lewis

Spiritual Pathways

A spiritual pathway has to do with the way we most naturally sense God's presence and experience spiritual growth. We all have at least one pathway that comes most easily to us. We also have one or two that are the most unnatural and require stretching for us to pursue. There is enormous freedom in identifying and embracing your personal spiritual pathway. You can focus on relating to God in that way for which you were made, while at the same time recognizing your need to stretch in certain areas that don't come as naturally.

In what ways are you comfortable with the person God made you to be? In what ways are you trying to be like someone God made differently?

Intellectual Pathway

If you're on the intellectual pathway, the road to your heart usually runs through your head. You hear God best when you learn. You need to continually immerse yourself in great books, deep thoughts, and sound teaching. When your mind is growing, you feel fully alive. Many of your most significant moments of worship or devotion or decision or repentance came when you were in deep learning mode. You may want to sign up for classes at a seminary or go online for distance learning or obtain tapes of a few great teachers.

Foundational Truth: God is *always* present and active in my life, whether or not I see him.

The danger of the intellectual pathway lies in becoming all head and no heart. Dallas Willard once observed that it is extremely difficult to be right and not to hurt anybody with it. Very few people enjoy sitting next to the kid in class who's right all the time—and knows it. One of the remarkable things about Jesus is that he was always right, yet he never damaged anyone with his mental superiority. "Knowledge puffs up, but love builds up," wrote Paul, who was in a good position to know. You may want to stretch by making sure your growth in knowledge always leads to a growth in worship.

How can you ensure that you will know the truth yet not hurt anyone with it?

Relational Pathway

People who follow the relational pathway find that they have a deep sense of God's presence when they're involved in significant relationships. People on this pathway need to lead a relationally rich life. They need to be part of friendships and small groups that are growing in depth and vulnerability. They will discover that they are much more likely to practice prayer or acts of servanthood when they can do it in a relational context. People on this pathway tend to hear God speak to them more in a conversation than from a book. They stagnate spiritually when they are isolated from other people.

Foundational Truth: Coming to recognize and experience God's presence is *learned* behavior; I can cultivate it.

Relational types always have to guard against two dangers. One is superficiality. It is possible to get spread so thin relationally that no one gets past your external self to know you, love you, and challenge you deeply. The second is to become so dependent on others that you live as a kind of spiritual chameleon. Practices like solitude and silence will be a stretch for you. They may never feel natural, but they will help free you from becoming addicted to what others think.

What practical steps can you take to guard against superficiality and overdependence on others?

Serving Pathway

On the serving pathway, people find that God's presence seems most tangible when they are involved in helping others. If this is you, you feel a sense of God's delight when you can do something—set up chairs, make coffee, help decorate. You often find yourself making observations that help you grow, or speaking to God in ways that feel most natural, while you are engaged in acts of service. People on this pathway need to be plugged into a community where they have meaningful serving opportunities. They can enrich their sense of God's presence in their lives by constantly looking for him in the people they serve.

Foundational Truth: My task is to meet God in *this* moment.

A danger to people on the serving pathway is the temptation to think God is present only when they are serving. They can get so caught up in being God's servant they forget that first of all, they are his child. They will have to stretch by learning to receive love as well as offer it. Another danger is that if they are a big-time server, they may be tempted to resent others who are not serving as much as they are.

How can you practice receiving love from others? How can you avoid resenting people who are not on the serving pathway, as Martha resented Mary in the story from Luke's gospel?

Worship Pathway

People on the worship pathway have a natural gift for expression and celebration. Something deep inside them feels released when praise and adoration are given voice. Some of their most formative moments occur during times of worship. If this is you, somehow in worship your heart opens up and you come alive. You sometimes find yourself in tears, sometimes in moments of deep joy, because God seems so close. If this is your pathway, you need to experience great worship on a regular basis.

Foundational Truth: I am always tempted to live "outside" this moment. When I do that, I lose my sense of God's presence.

Spiritual Pathways

Cautions for people on the worship pathway: Don't judge people who are not as outwardly expressive as you. Also, guard against an experienced-based spirituality that has you always looking for the next "worship high." It can lead you to worship an experience rather than the God to whom your experience points. Music, for instance, can be a great gift to worship. But you may need to spend some time worshiping God without music so that your worship is based on who God is and not a matter of getting swept up in certain sounds. Engaging in study will be an important stretch for you, so that your heart is deeply rooted in the knowledge of God.

In what ways might you worship God without music?

Activist Pathway

If you have an activist pathway, you have a passion to act. At the end of the day, you want to be able to pray, *I ran really hard today. I used every ounce of effort and zeal at my disposal, God, and it's all for you.* For activists, prayer and action naturally go together. They are triggered to look for and depend on God's presence and guidance in the heat of battle. If you are an activist, you need a cause. It doesn't have to be glamorous or visible, but it has to demand the best you have to offer.

Foundational Truth: Sometimes God seems far away for reasons I do not understand. Those moments, too, are opportunities to learn.

A caution for activists is that you may get so excited about the cause that you begin to run over other people or exploit them in order to accomplish your goal. Even God may become a means to an end for you rather than the One you serve. Activists sometimes have a hard time discerning God's true call from their own strong impulses to action. You may need to create balance by spending time in solitude and reflection, so that you allow God to speak to you about what is truly motivating your action.

How can you avoid abusing people in seeking to serve God?

Foundational Truth: Whenever I fail at recognizing and experiencing God's presence, I can always start again right away.

Contemplative Pathway

If you have a contemplative pathway, you love large blocks of uninterrupted time alone. Reflection comes naturally to you. God is most present to you when distractions and noises are removed. Images, metaphors, and pictures help you as you pray. Making time to listen to God in silence and solitude is vital to the health of your soul, and necessary for you to experience a deepening sense of his presence. Reading the work of other contemplatives, such as St. John of the Cross or Henri Nouwen, helps you, as does keeping a journal.

Foundational Truth: No one knows the full extent to which a human being can experience God's presence.

If you are a contemplative, you may need *permission* to follow your pathway. American society tends to value networkers and activists; contemplatives don't end up on many magazine covers. Also, you may need to stretch in the area of relationships. It will be tempting for you to retreat to your inner world when friends or work or society disappoints you. Involvement in significant relationships and regular acts of service will help keep you tethered to the external world.

If you are a contemplative person, from whom do you feel you need permission to follow your pathway?

Foundational Truth: My desire for God ebbs and flows, but his desire for me is constant.

Creation Pathway

Creation types find that they have a passionate ability to connect with God when they are experiencing the world he made. For people on the creation pathway, there is something deeply life-giving and God-breathed about nature. Being outdoors replenishes and energizes them, and opens their spirit to God. If creation is your pathway, you will want to spend large chunks of time outdoors. It will often be particularly helpful to have times of prayer or meditation in nature.

Foundational Truth: Every thought carries a "spiritual charge" that moves me a little closer to or a little farther from God.

Spiritual Pathways

People on the creation pathway may need to guard against using it as an escape. Human beings are part of creation, too—but you may find that when they disappoint you, you are tempted to run away to the woods. Folks in our day are sometimes prone to think, *I don't need church; I can worship God on my own in nature.* But of course, we have to learn to see beauty where God does, and people are the most valued creation of all.

How can you avoid using the creation pathway as an escape? How can you learn to see beauty in people, too?

Foundational Truth: My path to experiencing God's presence will not look quite like anyone else's.

Using the Pathways to Experience God

We need to accept and embrace the unique way God created us. Instead of following "mass production" approaches to spiritual growth, we need to make sure that we spend adequate time and activity pursuing the pathways that most help us connect with God. Understand and build on your pathways. Celebrate that this is part of how God made you and wants to connect with you. But also pay attention to those pathways that may not come naturally to you. It is important that you have some involvement in each of the pathways. No one should ignore their intellectual life or opt out of worship.

Foundational Truth: I can experience God's presence without straining and trying too hard.

God wants to have a relationship with you that is unlike his relationship with any other being in all creation. In the book of Revelation, John writes that one day we will each receive from God a name that remains a secret between him and us throughout eternity. "In my Father's house are many rooms," Jesus said. One of them was added when you became his child—no one else can ever occupy it. It is secret to you and him.

What qualities about your relationship with God feel unique and special to you?

Chapter 8

"As You Wish"

What matters, what Heaven desires and Hell fears, is precisely that further step, out of our depth, out of our own control.

C.S. Lewis

"As You Wish"

As You Wish

There is one line that lies at the heart of the book *The Princess Bride*—and at the heart of your story, as well. It is spoken when the story begins and when it ends. It is a kind of prayer. In fact, it is the greatest prayer Jesus himself ever prayed. If we were ever able to pray it truly and continually, it is in a real sense the only prayer you and I would ever need. "At the heart of communion with God," writes Gary Moon, "is the whisper, 'As you wish.'"

What inspires or motivates you to obey God?

Let us often remember, dear friend, that our sole occupation in life is to please God.

Brother Lawrence

"As You Wish"

For many centuries, those wisest among us about the spiritual life have insisted that this one line is the door that opens the heart to the presence of God. There is no greater expression of love than a freely submitted will. *As you wish.*

Jesus said, "As the Father has loved me, so have I loved you. Now remain in my love. If you obey my commands, you will remain in my love, just as I have obeyed my Father's commands and remain in his love."

John 15:9–10

Foundational Truth: God is *always* present and active in my life, whether or not I see him.

"As You Wish"

The heart that learns to say, "As you wish," opens itself to the Power of the Universe. It does not matter whether our task is great or small or whether we are famous or obscure. Anne Lamott has a wonderful thought: "The Gulf Stream can pass through a straw; if the straw aligns itself with the Gulf Stream."

How do you know when you are aligned with the Power of the Universe? What does it feel like? How do you adjust your alignment when you sense it is off?

Every moment, and in respect of everything, we must say like St. Paul, "Lord, what should I do? Let me do everything you wish."

Jean Pierre de Caussade

Conductors and Resisters

An analogy from the field of electricity can help us think about our response to God. The difference between a conductor and a resistor can be put like this: A conductor is willing to let go. Floating around the periphery of its atoms are electrons that can quite easily pass from one atom to another. So a conductor has what we might call a generosity of spirit when it comes to electrons. Ignatius of Loyola said we are to cultivate a sense of indifference. The idea is that our deepest desire is for God and his kind of life, and every other desire has to take a backseat to this one absolute quest.

Foundational Truth: Coming to recognize and experience God's presence is *learned* behavior; I can cultivate it.

"As You Wish"

The secret of the conductor is that it is not generating its own power. The conductor is not particularly strong or clever; it is simply a conduit. It is open and receptive to the flow of current that can change the world from darkness to light. We live in a spiritually charged universe. The flow of the Holy Spirit is all around us. We did not invent it, but it has now become fully available. Jesus once said, "Whoever believes in me, as Scripture has said, streams of living water will flow from within them."

What is faith, and how can you increase your faith in Jesus if it's not as strong as it should be?

Foundational Truth: My task is to meet God in *this* moment.

The Glow of the Pickle

I once did an electrical experiment in church. We turned off all the lights, hooked up an ordinary pickle to some wires, then passed an electrical current through it. The pickle glowed, giving light to thousands of people. Many people believe that the flow of the Holy Spirit is reserved for spiritual giants. But throughout history God has caused his power to flow through the most unlikely people. If God can make a pickle glow, what can he do through you?

Foundational Truth: I am always tempted to live "outside" this moment. When I do that, I lose my sense of God's presence.

"As You Wish"

It is God's job to send the flow of the Spirit into our lives. When we have thoughts that prompt us toward the fruit of the Spirit—promptings to express love to someone, celebrations of inner joy, the conviction that we are at peace—these are all surges of the Spirit's current. Our job, in a sense, is to offer the surrender of a conductor. *As you wish.*

What specific disciplines can you put into place to ensure the Spirit's power flows through you?

Foundational Truth: Sometimes God seems far away for reasons I do not understand. Those moments, too, are opportunities to learn.

The Surrender of Obedience

While traveling overseas, I noticed that the television in my hotel room listed an "adults-only" channel that was free of charge. I asked one of the men on the trip to hold me accountable not to watch the channel. He later told me about a vulnerable issue in *his* life that we would never have discussed if I hadn't taken a first step of vulnerability. God used this man in my life, and me in his, in a way neither of us could have foreseen.

Foundational Truth: I can experience God's presence without straining and trying too hard.

"As You Wish"

The Surrender of Paying Attention

The same God who is within us is also all around us. When we see beauty that overwhelms us; when we see acts of compassion that make us choke up; when we feel longing so deep and sweet that everything else in our life recedes; when the turn of a phrase or a bar of music catches us off guard and takes our breath away—it may be more than just an aesthetic experience. It may be God within us, indwelling every cell in our body, calling out for us to see and open ourselves up to his presence.

Foundational Truth: No one knows the full extent to which a human being can experience God's presence.

"As You Wish"

Our task, in order to stay in the flow of God's presence, is to pay attention. To refuse the blindness that comes with self-preoccupation. To allow the God who is in us to point to and rejoice in his presence all around us. To ask him to keep us from sleepwalking through his world; to refuse to give in to a pace of life that reduces his handiwork to a blur. We do not need to hunt for God. We only need to open our eyes.

How does self-preoccupation blind you to God's presence?

We are here to abet Creation and to witness it, to notice each thing, so each thing gets noticed ... so that Creation need not play to an empty house.

Anne Dillard

"As You Wish"

One Thing Surrender Is Not

The call to surrender does not mean we are to kill off all our desires. God created desire. In his original plan, desires are an indicator of a creature's purpose. Distorted spirituality says real life requires the elimination of our desires. Jesus says that real life requires the transformation of our desires. If you are thirsty—if you have unsatisfied desires—"come to me." Desire itself is an invitation to seek God's presence.

If we consider ... the staggering nature of the rewards promised in the Gospels, it would seem that Our Lord finds our desires, not too strong, but too weak.... We are far too easily pleased.

C.S. Lewis

The Surrender of Our Failures

Since my family moved to northern California, we have become surfing addicts. The good news about surfing is this: If you miss one wave, if you fall off, if you wipe out, there's another wave right behind it. God just keeps sending them. He never runs out of waves. He has an inexhaustible supply. He's like a wave machine. The Bible's word for that is grace. Even when we have failed, the flow of the Spirit can be restored in our lives at any moment. Right now. All we have to do is ask.

What makes it hard for you to ask for God's grace?

Foundational Truth: My desire for God ebbs and flows, but his desire for me is constant.

Chapter 9

When God Seems Absent

This eternal fountain is
hidden deep,
Well I know where it has
its spring,
Though it is night!
St. John of the Cross

When God Seems Absent

You can relocate to another part of the world to avoid cold weather, but there is no place you can move to escape spiritual winter. Theologian Martin E. Marty wrote a book of reflections about the terminal illness and death of his beloved wife. He said one of the resources human beings need is a "wintry spirituality" for times when warmth and joy are taken from us and a sunny disposition is not enough to bring them back. We need a way of holding on to God when it feels as if God has let go of us.

How can you build up a "wintry spirituality"?

Foundational Truth: God is *always* present and active in my life, whether or not I see him.

When God Seems Absent

Job and the Absence of God

In all of human history, no one has embodied winter more than a man named Job. In his book we come to the page where Waldo is hardest to find. His problems are the problems of the human race. All of us will wrestle at some time with the absence of God. The question is, can a human being hold on to God in the face of suffering? After all, suffering is the test of love.

Foundational Truth: Coming to recognize and experience God's presence is *learned* behavior; I can cultivate it.

Friends in Winter

Job's friends hear about all his troubles. Their love is so strong, their grief is so great, that they plan to sit next to him and take on his anguish. This incident is perhaps the greatest example in Scripture of what Paul commands in Romans: "Mourn with those who mourn." Maybe the best way to mediate God's presence to someone who is suffering is to sit with them in silence.

In what other ways can you, without using words, allow God's Spirit to flow through you and minister to someone who is suffering?

Foundational Truth: My task is to meet God in *this* moment.

The Doctrine of Retribution

We generally associate well-being with the presence of God, and assume that suffering means someone has done something wrong. Of course, it is true that pain was not part of God's original plan, and the day is coming when he will wipe every tear from our eyes. And yet, while God hates pain, he can also redeem it. It does not mean he is absent.

Foundational Truth: My path to experiencing God's presence will not look quite like anyone else's.

Mini-Pain

One thing we can do is practice God's presence in moments of "mini-pain." Suppose I'm frustrated at standing in line at a 7-Eleven store. That's maybe a "1" on a pain scale of 1,000, but I can, in a sense, use it as a tool. I can ask God to be present with me in my frustration. I can look for him in the clerk behind the counter who doesn't speak English very well. The practice of walking with God in mini-pain can serve people well when larger pain comes.

Into what mini-painful situations will you begin inviting God?

Foundational Truth: Sometimes God seems far away for reasons I do not understand. Those moments, too, are opportunities to learn.

When God Seems Absent

Almost six years ago, I had the most painful year of my life. Over time, I came to see that it was doing much good in me. I became much more aware of how everything meaningful in life rides on God. Certain temptations became much less seductive; spiritual reality got clearer. Pain brings gifts from God that nothing else can. It can cause me to wonder where God is, as nothing else can. And it can open me up to my dependence on his presence, as nothing else can.

Foundational Truth: Whenever I fail at recognizing and experiencing God's presence, I can always start again right away.

The Gift of Complaining

Israelites devoted more psalms to complaining than any other single category. These prayers of complaint are powerful—and an important part of our own spiritual life. When we are passionately honest with God, when we are not indulging in self-pity or martyrdom, but are genuinely opening ourselves up to God, when we complain in hope that God can still be trusted—then we are asking God to create the kind of condition in our heart that will make resting in his presence possible again.

How can you keep your prayers of complaint from turning into grumbling, which God condemns?

Foundational Truth: I can experience God's presence without straining and trying too hard.

The Kind of Person God Is

Ellen Davis writes that God's questions to Job indicate something about the kind of Person he is. They are filled with references to his extravagant goodness and provision. God is a God of gratuitous goodness. He is uncontrollably generous. He is irrationally loving. He is good just because he loves to give. What God is really telling Job is, "I'm worth it. Life, following me—it's all worth it. Don't give up. This pain is not going to last forever. *I am the kind of God who is worth getting close to.*"

Foundational Truth: My desire for God ebbs and flows, but his desire for me is constant.

"Man of Sorrows"

When God himself came to the earth, he came in winter. Jesus, like Job, was known as a "man of sorrows." He was acquainted with grief. The cross demonstrates the ultimate paradox: God experiencing the absence of God so that he can draw close to us in our loss, grief, and God-forsakenness. If it is winter in your life, you don't have to wonder where God is. He is there with you.

In what specific ways do you think Jesus can relate to what you are suffering right now?

Foundational Truth: Every thought carries a "spiritual charge" that moves me a little closer to or a little farther from God.

When God Seems Absent

The central question in Job is, can a human being hold on to God, faith, and love even in the dead of winter? One can. One did. Job did not know that his faithfulness had meaning beyond his wildest dreams. He did not know that something cosmic and eternal was at stake in his transitory life. But Job discovered what people in pain sometimes learn better than anyone else. He was not alone after all. Not even in winter.

Foundational Truth: Every aspect of my life—work, relationships, hobbies, errands—is of immense and genuine interest to God.

Chapter 10

The Hedge

Discernment is like driving an automobile at night; the headlights cast only enough light for us to see the next small bit of road immediately in front of us. But that light is enough to take us home.

Suzanne Farnham

The Hedge

Outside my door is a backyard called the Universe. And at the border of the universe is a hedge. The hedge is a barrier that traps me in the aloneness of my backyard and cuts me off from a larger Presence. Some people are convinced that there is Nothing behind the hedge, that our backyard is all there is. But the whispers and rumors of the Presence are curiously stubborn. There seems to be in the human race an irrepressible instinct that Something lies behind the hedge, that there is more to existence than a swirl of molecules and atoms, that death is a gate and not a fence, that reality is bigger than just our backyard.

What convinces you that Something lies beyond the hedge?

Thin Places

Philip Yancey writes that “Celtic spirituality speaks of ‘thin places’ where the natural and supernatural worlds come together at their narrowest.” The birth of a child, the words to an ancient hymn, the sight of the sun rising over the rim of a sleeping world—the thin places can be as momentous as life and death or as tiny as the rustle of a hummingbird’s wings. For some people the veil seems to be thinner than others—a hairbreadth, like the space between Adam and God in the Sistine Chapel.

Foundational Truth: God is *always* present and active in my life, whether or not I see him.

The Hedge

What is behind the hedge? It is ironic that the keenest minds in the world spend their lives thinking and probing and studying to answer this one question and never know for sure, yet the biggest fool in the universe knows one second after he dies. You find out for sure—or there's no you anymore to find out anything—one second after it's too late to do anything about it. I almost always have this thought when I hear of someone who has died: *Now he knows.*

Do you believe it is possible to know with certainty, in this lifetime, what is behind the hedge? Why or why not?

Foundational Truth: Coming to recognize and experience God's presence is learned behavior; I can cultivate it.

The Hedge

Those who believe that Something lies behind the hedge must struggle with why the hedge is there at all. Why does the Something stay so hidden? Does the hedge serve a purpose? Is it possible that there is some good in not knowing? Those who believe that Nothing lies behind the hedge must struggle with why the rumors of Something are so persistent. Harder still, they must struggle with what to do during their brief time in the backyard if the backyard turns out to be nothing more than a cemetery.

Foundational Truth: I am always tempted to live "outside" this moment. When I do that, I lose my sense of God's presence.

The Hedge

One day a man who looked like all other men made a breathtaking claim. He said he came from the other side of the hedge. He said no one has to be alone anymore. No one has to live in fear. He said a new kind of life—life "with-God"—is now available to anyone who wants it. And he didn't bring this life just to give us comfort. He brought it to give us a mission. He said anyone who enters this life will join him in becoming carriers of it to others in the backyard.

In what ways can you enjoy the comfort of the life Jesus brings, while accepting its mission, as well?

Foundational Truth: My task is to meet God in *this* moment.

The Hedge-Breaker

There has been a fundamental misunderstanding about Jesus' message in our day. People have gotten the idea that Jesus' gospel—his Good News—is primarily about how to get ready for life on the other side of the hedge, rather than the announcement that the mysterious Someone has broken through the hedge and entered our own backyard. This misunderstanding has had the devastating consequence of keeping many people from seeking to *experience* God's presence in their lives here and now.

Foundational Truth: Sometimes God seems far away for reasons I do not understand. Those moments, too, are opportunities to learn.

The Hedge

When we look closely at what Jesus calls his good news, he does not put it in terms of something that happens after you die. He speaks of something that happens on this side of the hedge. The good news Jesus announced was simply this: God has invaded our backyard and is making his presence and power available to anybody who wants him. Right here. Right now. "The time has come," Jesus says. God is really closer than you think.

How can you change your thinking to begin viewing the gospel more as something that relates to this life, as well as the next?

Foundational Truth: Whenever I fail at recognizing and experiencing God's presence, I can always start again right away.

The Hedge

Jesus' gospel includes forgiveness of our sins as a gift of grace. It includes the promise that death will not have the last word, that our eternal life with God will never cease. But it includes more than that. The promise fulfilled in Jesus' coming is the unifying theme of Scripture: *Immanuel*, "God with us." Jesus said, "Anyone who loves me will obey my teaching. My Father will love them, and we will come to them and *make our home with them.*"

Foundational Truth: No one knows the full extent to which a human being can experience God's presence.

Jacob's Ladder Revisited

At the beginning of his ministry, Jesus explained his mission to a man named Nathanael: "I tell you the truth, you shall see heaven open, and the angels of God ascending and descending on the Son of Man." Jesus is referring, of course, to Jacob's vision. Jesus himself came as "Jacob's ladder" that now reaches down to your life and mine. Many people think the only real reason Jesus came to earth was to die on the cross. But death on the cross was just one part of his mission. His overall mission was to bring the reality of God's presence and power to our side of the hedge.

To what extent has Jesus succeeded with his overall mission in your life?

Make "Up There" Come Down Here

Jesus told us to pray, "Bring heaven down here." We begin with our bodies, our minds, our appetites. Then it spreads to the office, our families, our neighborhoods, our churches, our countries. God doesn't reveal himself to us just to make us happy or to deliver us from loneliness. He also comes to us so that we can, in turn, be conduits of his presence to other people. He invites us to join him in making things down here the way they are up there.

Foundational Truth: I can experience God's presence without straining and trying too hard.

The Hedge

A Place to Start

Start by asking yourself this question: "Where do I want to see God's presence and power break into my world? Where would I especially like God to use me to make things down here run the way they do up there?"

Our Father in heaven,
hallowed be your name,
your kingdom come,
your will be done
on earth as it is in heaven.

Matthew 6:9–10

Foundational Truth: Every thought carries a "spiritual charge" that moves me a little closer to or a little farther from God.

The Hedge

Internally, most of us want to experience the *feelings* of God's presence: a deeper sense of peace and assurance, a stronger surge of joy, a clearer word of guidance. Is it possible for the practice of the presence of God to become a thinly veiled pursuit of emotional comfort? Ironically, none of these feelings are necessary for us to become agents of God's presence for other people. All that is necessary is a single intent: *Lord, where do you want to use me to help things down here run the way they do up there?*

Foundational Truth: Every aspect of my life—work, relationships, hobbies, errands—is of immense and genuine interest to God.

God at the DMV

There is no place where God's presence cannot break through to you. I was in the Department of Motor Vehicles. The elderly woman in front of me was taking forever. Then the prayer came to me: *God, make things down here like they are up there*. Immediately the thought occurred to me, *I could go over and see if I can help that woman*. For a few moments, I got to help the kingdom of love be present to someone who needed it. For a few moments, God's kingdom broke into the DMV.

For whom will you start praying, *Lord, bring heaven down here?*

God's Costly Presence

Every time you are in conflict with someone and then go to them and seek reconciliation and forgiveness—the kingdom is breaking into this world. Every time you decide to give sacrificially to somebody who is hungry or homeless or poor—the kingdom is breaking into the world. Every time you love, every time you include someone who's lonely, every time you encourage someone who's defeated—it is a sign that the kingdom is once more breaking into the world.

How can you cooperate with God's work in you, so that it can spread all the more quickly throughout your life?

Sources:

Chapter 1

Thomas Kelly, *A Testament of Devotion*. San Francisco: HarperSanFrancisco, 1992, 90.

Frederick Buechner, *Listening to Your Life*. San Francisco: HarperSanFrancisco, 1992, 2.

Chapter 2

Armand Nicholi, *The Question of God*. Quoted in Karen Mains, The God Hunt. Downers Grove, IL: InterVarsity Press, 2003, 13.

William Barry, *Finding God in All Things*. Notre Dame, IN: Ave Maria Press, 1991, 14–15.

Chapter 3

J. D. Salinger, *Franny and Zooey*. New York: Bantam Books, 1964, 170.

Chapter 4

William Blake, "Auguries of Innocence."

Frederick Buechner, *The Alphabet of Grace*. New York: Harper & Row, 1970, 12.

Brother Lawrence, *Practicing the Presence of God*. Springdale, PA: Whitaker House, 1982, 31.

Chapter 5

Frank Laubach, *Letters by a Modern Mystic*. Old Tappan, NJ: Revell, 1958.

John Calvin, *Institutes of the Christian Religion*, book I, ch. 13, sect. 1.

Chapter 6

Esther de Waal, *Seeking God: The Way of St. Benedict*. Collegeville, MN: Liturgical Press, 1984, 126.

Frank Laubach, *Man of Prayer*. Syracuse, NY: Laubach Literacy International, 1990, 329–30.

Chapter 7

C. S. Lewis, The *Problem of Pain*. Reprint: New York: HarperCollins, 2001, 154.

Chapter 8

C. S. Lewis, "A Slip of the Tongue," in *The Weight of Glory*. New York: Macmillan, 1980, 131.

Jean Pierre de Caussade, *The Sacrament of the Present Moment*. Translated by Kitty Muggeridge. San Francisco: Harper & Row, 1982: Quoted in Richard J. Foster and James Bryan Smith, eds., *Devotional Classics*. San Francisco: HarperSanFrancisco, 1993, 232.

Anne Dillard, in an essay first appearing in *Life* magazine and later included in *The Meaning of Life*, ed. David Friend and the editors of *Life*. Boston: Little Brown, 1991.

Lewis, *The Weight of Glory*, 3.

Chapter 9

St. John of the Cross: "Song of the Soul that delights in knowing God by faith," from *St. John of the Cross: Alchemist of the Soul: His Life, His Poetry, His Prose*. Edited by Antonia T. De Nicholas. York Beach, ME: Samuel Weiser, 1989, 131.

Chapter 10

Suzanne Farnham et al., *Listening Hearts: Discerning Call in Community*. Harrisburg, PA: Morehouse Publishing, 1991, 27.